THE LITTLE BOOK OF
BOOKS

Published in 2022 by OH!
An Imprint of Welbeck Non-Fiction Limited,
part of Welbeck Publishing Group.
Based in London and Sydney.
www.welbeckpublishing.com

Compilation text © Welbeck Non-Fiction Limited 2022
Design © Welbeck Non-Fiction Limited 2022

Disclaimer:
All trademarks, quotations, company names, registered names, individual names, products, logos and catchphrases used or cited in this book are the property of their respective owners and used in this book for informational, reporting, review and guidance purposes only. This book is a publication of *OH! An imprint of Welbeck Publishing Group Limited* and has not been licensed, approved, sponsored, or endorsed by any person or entity.

All rights reserved. No part of this publication may be reproduced, stored in a retrieval system, or transmitted in any form or by any means (including electronic, mechanical, photocopying, recording, or otherwise) without prior written permission from the publisher.

ISBN 978-1-80069-174-2

Compiled and written by: Marcus Leaver
Editorial: Stella Caldwell
Project manager: Russell Porter
Design: Tony Seddon
Production: Jess Brisley

A CIP catalogue record for this book is available from the British Library

Printed in China

10 9 8 7 6 5 4 3 2 1

Illustrations: Freepik.com

THE LITTLE BOOK OF
BOOKS

QUOTES FOR THE BIBLIOPHILE
IN YOUR LIFE

CONTENTS

INTRODUCTION - 7

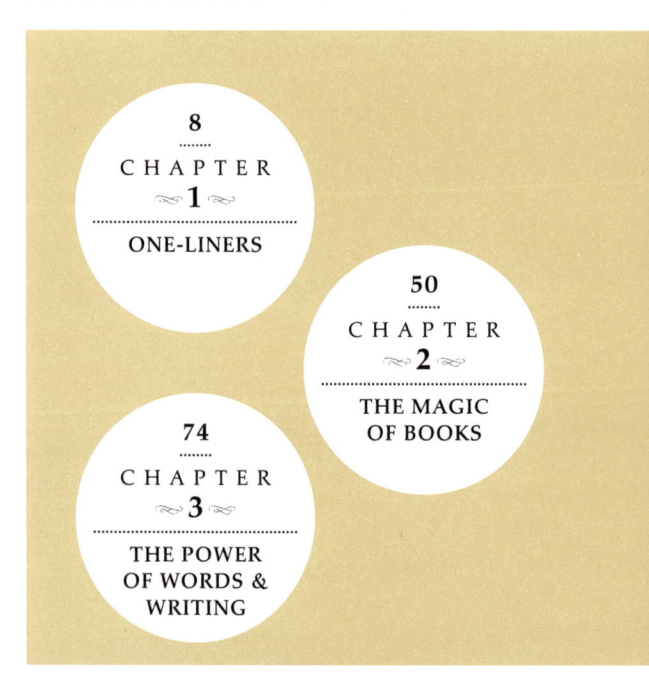

8
CHAPTER
1
ONE-LINERS

50
CHAPTER
2
THE MAGIC OF BOOKS

74
CHAPTER
3
THE POWER OF WORDS & WRITING

102

CHAPTER **4**

A PRECIOUS GIFT

136

CHAPTER **5**

MIRRORS OF THE SOUL

162

CHAPTER **6**

FAMOUS LINES FROM FAMOUS BOOKS

THE LITTLE BOOK OF BOOKS

*This book is dedicated to Henry,
a dear friend, who was
amused by the choice of author
and this publication.*

INTRODUCTION

Dear Book Lover

It was a joy to collate more than 200 one-liners, quotes about books, and great lines from great works to put into this small but perfectly formed little book about books and reading. I have enjoyed every minute of choosing what to include and what to discard.

Of course, this book is just my take on the subject and the pleasure it gives me. As with any curation, you will be pleased to revisit some much-loved lines, and disappointed that others you closely identify with have been left out. But hopefully, the bibliophile will find something contained within these pages to delight them, inspire them or have them buy another book, for themselves or as a gift for someone dear to them.

HAPPY READING.

Marcus E. Leaver
London
July 2021

CHAPTER

1

One-liners

Do you live for books? Do you believe that a room without books is like a body without a soul? Do you think books should be tasted….?

What follows are some of my favourite quotes by some of the most famous people who have ever lived and written.

THE LITTLE BOOK OF BOOKS

We live for books.

Umberto Eco

ONE-LINERS

> Books are a uniquely portable magic.

Stephen King

THE LITTLE BOOK OF BOOKS

"

A room without books is like a body without a soul.

"

Cicero

ONE-LINERS

> Good friends, good books, and a sleepy conscience: this is the ideal life.

Mark Twain

THE LITTLE BOOK OF BOOKS

> Books serve to show a man that those original thoughts of his aren't very new after all.

Abraham Lincoln

ONE-LINERS

> Some books should be tasted, some devoured, but only a few should be chewed and digested thoroughly.

Sir Francis Bacon

THE LITTLE BOOK OF BOOKS

> # Let us read and let us dance; these two amusements will never do any harm to the world.

Voltaire

ONE-LINERS

> You cannot open a book without learning something.

Confucius

THE LITTLE BOOK OF BOOKS

Read the best books first, or you may not have a chance to read them at all.

Henry David Thoreau

ONE-LINERS

66

Classic – a book which people praise and don't read.

99

Mark Twain

THE LITTLE BOOK OF BOOKS

Books are the training weights of the mind.

Epictetus

ONE-LINERS

"

I have never known any distress that an hour's reading did not relieve.

Montesquieu

THE LITTLE BOOK OF BOOKS

To read without reflecting is like eating without digesting.

Edmund Burke

ONE-LINERS

> **The most technologically efficient machine that man has ever invented is the book.**

Northrop Frye

THE LITTLE BOOK OF BOOKS

A book is a gift you can open again and again.

Garrison Keillor

ONE-LINERS

To learn to read
is to light a fire;
every syllable
that is spelled out
is a spark.

Victor Hugo

THE LITTLE BOOK OF BOOKS

A house without books is like a room without windows.

Heinrich Mann

ONE-LINERS

> Show me a family of readers, and I will show you the people who move the world.

Napoleon Bonaparte

THE LITTLE BOOK OF BOOKS

No entertainment is so cheap as reading, nor any pleasure so lasting.

Mary Wortley Montagu

ONE-LINERS

> The reading of all good books is like a conversation with the finest minds of past centuries.

René Descartes

THE LITTLE BOOK OF BOOKS

That's the thing about books. They let you travel without moving your feet.

Jhumpa Lahiri

ONE-LINERS

66
A reader lives a thousand lives before he dies.
99

George R.R. Martin

THE LITTLE BOOK OF BOOKS

> *I do believe something very magical can happen when you read a good book.*

J.K. Rowling

ONE-LINERS

> # "
> # The only thing you absolutely have to know is the location of the library.
> # "

Albert Einstein

THE LITTLE BOOK OF BOOKS

> " An hour spent reading is one stolen from paradise. "

Thomas Wharton

ONE-LINERS

> Reading is an active, imaginative act; it takes work.

Khaled Hosseini

> People don't realize how a man's whole life can be changed by one book.

Malcolm X

Of all things, I liked books best.

Nikola Tesla

THE LITTLE BOOK OF BOOKS

> # I kept always two books in my pocket, one to read, one to write in.

Robert Louis Stevenson

ONE-LINERS

> **Think before you speak, read before you think.**
>
> *Fran Lebowitz*

> Only a generation of readers will spawn a generation of writers.

Steven Spielberg

ONE-LINERS

> Once you have read a book you care about, some part of it is always with you.

Louis L'Amour

> Not all readers are leaders, but all leaders are readers.

Harry S. Truman

ONE-LINERS

> The world is a hellish place, and bad writing is destroying the quality of our suffering.

Tom Waits

THE LITTLE BOOK OF BOOKS

> Beware the person of a single book.

Thomas Aquinas

ONE-LINERS

> Reading is to the mind what exercise is to the body.

Joseph Addison

> The person who deserves most pity is a lonesome one on a rainy day who doesn't know how to read.

Benjamin Franklin

ONE-LINERS

> A book is a device to ignite the imagination.

Alan Bennett

THE LITTLE BOOK OF BOOKS

> # A good book is an event in my life.

Stendhal

ONE-LINERS

> **I think books are like people, in the sense that they'll turn up in your life when you most need them.**
>
> *Emma Thompson*

CHAPTER

2

The Magic of Books

*Books are truly magical.
They can entertain you, inspire
you, educate you – and,
always, they can enrich your
life in some way.*

*Some wise words follow about
that very magic.*

THE LITTLE BOOK OF BOOKS

> Books may well be the only true magic.

Alice Hoffman

THE MAGIC OF BOOKS

> A great book should leave you with many experiences, and slightly exhausted at the end. You live several lives while reading.

William Styron

THE LITTLE BOOK OF BOOKS

> In the case of good books, the point is not to see how many of them you can get through, but rather how many can get through to you.

Mortimer J. Adler

THE MAGIC OF BOOKS

> I can never read all the books I want; I can never be all the people I want and live all the lives I want. I can never train myself in all the skills I want. And why do I want?
> I want to live and feel all the shades, tones and variations of mental and physical experience possible in my life. And I am horribly limited.

Sylvia Plath

THE LITTLE BOOK OF BOOKS

> "
> Whenever you read a good book, somewhere in the world a door opens to allow in more light.
> "
>
> *Vera Nazarian*

THE MAGIC OF BOOKS

> Second-hand books are wild books, homeless books; they have come together in vast flocks of variegated feather and have a charm which the domesticated volumes of the library lack.

Virginia Woolf

> It is not true that we have only one life to live; if we can read, we can live as many more lives and as many kinds of lives as we wish.

S.I. Hayakawa

> We don't need a list of rights and wrongs, tables of dos and don'ts: we need books, time, and silence. Thou shalt not is soon forgotten, but Once upon a time lasts forever.

Philip Pullman

> Books and doors are the same thing. You open them, and you go through into another world.

Jeanette Winterson

THE MAGIC OF BOOKS

> Of course, anyone who truly loves books buys more of them than he or she can hope to read in one fleeting lifetime. A good book, resting unopened in its slot on a shelf, full of majestic potentiality, is the most comforting sort of intellectual wallpaper.

David Quammen

> I'm old-fashioned and think that reading books is the most glorious pastime that humankind has yet devised.

Wisława Szymborska

THE MAGIC OF BOOKS

> Read a lot. Expect something big, something exalting or deepening from a book. No book is worth reading that isn't worth re-reading.

Susan Sontag

THE LITTLE BOOK OF BOOKS

> There is nothing more luxurious than eating while you read – unless it be reading while you eat.

E. Nesbit

THE MAGIC OF BOOKS

> Man reading should be man intensely alive. The book should be a ball of light in one's hand.

Ezra Pound

THE LITTLE BOOK OF BOOKS

> Books are not made for furniture, but there is nothing else that so beautifully furnishes a house.

Henry Ward Beecher

> Books are the quietest and most constant of friends; they are the most accessible and wisest of counsellors, and the most patient of teachers.

Charles William Eliot

> Just the knowledge that a good book is awaiting one at the end of a long day makes that day happier.

Kathleen Norris

THE MAGIC OF BOOKS

> If you would tell me the heart of a man, tell me not what he reads, but what he re-reads.

François Mauriac

> Many people, myself among them, feel better at the mere sight of a book.

Jane Smiley

THE MAGIC OF BOOKS

> When we are collecting books, we are collecting happiness.

Vincent Starrett

> Everything in the world exists in order to end up as a book.

Stéphane Mallarmé

THE MAGIC OF BOOKS

It does not do to dwell on dreams and forget to live.

J.K. Rowling,
Harry Potter and The Sorcerer's Stone

CHAPTER 3

The Power of Words and Writing

Writing is never as easy as it seems. But books are knowledge, books are reflection and books change your mind.

Some celebrated authors explain why.

> Books are a form of political action. Books are knowledge. Books are reflection. Books change your mind.

Toni Morrison

THE POWER OF WORDS AND WRITING

> A word after a word after a word is power.

Margaret Atwood

> Despite the enormous quantity of books, how few people read! And if one reads profitably, one would realize how much stupid stuff the vulgar herd is content to swallow every day.

Voltaire

THE POWER OF WORDS AND WRITING

> Writing books is the closest men ever come to childbearing.

Norman Mailer

THE LITTLE BOOK OF BOOKS

> To produce a mighty book, you must choose a mighty theme.

Herman Melville

THE POWER OF WORDS AND WRITING

> A blank piece of paper is God's way of telling us how hard it is to be God.

Sidney Sheldon

> I love deadlines. I like the whooshing sound they make as they fly by.

Douglas Adams

THE POWER OF WORDS AND WRITING

> "
>
> There is no greater agony than bearing an untold story inside you.
>
> "

Maya Angelou

> The English language is an arsenal of weapons. If you are going to brandish them without checking to see whether or not they are loaded, you must expect to have them explode in your face from time to time.

Stephen Fry

THE POWER OF WORDS AND WRITING

> If my doctor told me I had only six minutes to live, I wouldn't brood. I'd type a little faster.

Isaac Asimov

THE LITTLE BOOK OF BOOKS

> Reading is my inhale, and writing is my exhale.

Glennon Doyle

> There are three rules for writing the novel. Unfortunately, no one knows what they are.

W. Somerset Maugham

> No tears in the writer, no tears in the reader. No surprise in the writer, no surprise in the reader.

Robert Frost

THE POWER OF WORDS AND WRITING

> A writer only begins a book. A reader finishes it.

Samuel Johnson

THE LITTLE BOOK OF BOOKS

> # Reading is the finest teacher of how to write.

Annie Proulx

> Libraries will get you through times of no money better than money will get you through times of no libraries.

Anne Herbert

> I couldn't live a week without a private library – indeed, I'd part with all my furniture and squat and sleep on the floor before I'd let go of the 1,500 or so books, I possess.

H. P. Lovecraft

> When I am attacked by gloomy thoughts, nothing helps me so much as running to my books. They quickly absorb me and banish the clouds from my mind.

Michel de Montaigne

> Words dazzle and deceive because they are mimed by the face. But black words on a white page are the soul laid bare.

Guy de Maupassant

THE POWER OF WORDS AND WRITING

> Even today, when I read, I notice with pleasure when an author has chosen a particular word, a particular place, for the picture it will convey to the reader.

Ruth Bader Ginsburg

> I don't believe one reads to escape reality. A person reads to confirm a reality he knows is there, but which he has not experienced.

Lawrence Durrell

> Do not read, as children do, to amuse yourself, or like the ambitious, for the purpose of instruction. No, read in order to live.

Gustave Flaubert

> Employ your time in improving yourself by other men's writings so that you shall come easily by what others have laboured hard for.

Socrates

THE POWER OF WORDS AND WRITING

> I know nothing in the world that has as much power as a word. Sometimes I write one, and I look at it, until it begins to shine.

Emily Dickinson

THE LITTLE BOOK OF BOOKS

> The best advice I ever got was that knowledge is power and to keep reading.

David Bailey

THE POWER OF WORDS AND WRITING

> Beware; for I am fearless, and therefore powerful.

Mary Shelley, Frankenstein

CHAPTER 4

A Precious Gift

A child who is read to or receives a book will never see reading as a chore but as a precious gift.

And when that child grows into an adult, they can keep that precious gift for life.

THE LITTLE BOOK OF BOOKS

> Reading should not be presented to children as a chore or duty. It should be offered to them as a precious gift.

Kate DiCamillo

A PRECIOUS GIFT

> A children's story that can only be enjoyed by children is not a good children's story in the slightest.

C.S. Lewis

THE LITTLE BOOK OF BOOKS

> I wouldn't be a songwriter if it wasn't for books that I loved as a kid. I think that when you can escape into a book it trains your imagination to think big and to think that more can exist than what you see.

Taylor Swift

A PRECIOUS GIFT

> Reading is the gateway skill that makes all other learning possible.

Barack Obama

THE LITTLE BOOK OF BOOKS

> There are many little ways to enlarge your child's world. Love of books is the best of all.

Jacqueline Kennedy

A PRECIOUS GIFT

> Once you learn to read, you will be forever free.

Frederick Douglass

THE LITTLE BOOK OF BOOKS

> There are perhaps no days of our childhood we lived so fully as those we spent with a favourite book.

Marcel Proust

A PRECIOUS GIFT

> One child, one teacher, one book and one pen can change the world.

Malala Yousafzai

THE LITTLE BOOK OF BOOKS

> Reading is important, because if you can read, you can learn anything about everything and everything about anything.

Tomie dePaola

A PRECIOUS GIFT

> I have a passion for teaching kids to become readers, to become comfortable with a book, not daunted. Books shouldn't be daunting, they should be funny, exciting and wonderful; and learning to be a reader gives a terrific advantage.

Roald Dahl

THE LITTLE BOOK OF BOOKS

> Books to the ceiling,
> Books to the sky,
> My pile of books is a mile high.
> How I love them!
> How I need them!
> I'll have a long beard by the time I read them.

Arnold Lobel

A PRECIOUS GIFT

> Fairy tales don't tell children that dragons exist… Fairy tales tell children that dragons can be killed.

G.K. Chesterton

THE LITTLE BOOK OF BOOKS

> "
>
> There is no substitute for books in the life of a child.
>
> "

Mary Ellen Chase

A PRECIOUS GIFT

> There's no such thing as a kid who hates reading. There are kids who love reading, and kids who are reading the wrong books.

James Patterson

THE LITTLE BOOK OF BOOKS

> If you want your children to be intelligent, read them fairy tales. If you want them to be more intelligent, read them more fairy tales.

Albert Einstein

A PRECIOUS GIFT

> Always read something that will make you look good if you die in the middle of it.

P.J. O'Rourke

> Outside of a dog, a book is man's best friend. Inside of a dog it's too dark to read.

Groucho Marx, The Essential Groucho

A PRECIOUS GIFT

> Fill your house with stacks of books, in all the crannies and all the nooks.

Dr. Seuss

> There are two motives for reading a book: one, that you enjoy it; the other, that you can boast about it.

Bertrand Russell, The Conquest of Happiness

A PRECIOUS GIFT

> A bookstore is one of the many pieces of evidence we have that people are still thinking.

Jerry Seinfeld

THE LITTLE BOOK OF BOOKS

> Let's be reasonable and add an eighth day to the week that is devoted exclusively to reading.

Lena Dunham

A PRECIOUS GIFT

> To a soul attuned to the subtle rhythms of a library, there are few worse sights than a hole where a book ought to be.

Terry Pratchett

> Never lend books, for no one ever returns them; the only books I have in my library are books that other folks have lent me.

Anatole France

A PRECIOUS GIFT

> I love walking into a bookstore. It's like all my friends are sitting on shelves, waving their pages at me.

Tahereh Mafi

> Take a good book to bed with you – books do not snore.

Thea Dorn

A PRECIOUS GIFT

> **What I say is, a town isn't a town without a bookstore. It may call itself a town, but unless it's got a bookstore, it knows it's not foolin' a soul.**

Neil Gaiman, American Gods

> There are books of which the backs and covers are by far the best parts.

Charles Dickens, Oliver Twist

A PRECIOUS GIFT

> The reason that fiction is more interesting than any other form of literature, to those who really like to study people, is that in fiction the author can really tell the truth without humiliating himself.

Eleanor Roosevelt

: THE LITTLE BOOK OF BOOKS

> Where is human nature so weak as in the bookstore?

Henry Ward Beecher

A PRECIOUS GIFT

> I read my eyes out and can't read half enough… The more one reads the more one sees we have to read.

John Adams

THE LITTLE BOOK OF BOOKS

> People can lose their lives in libraries. They ought to be warned.

Saul Bellow

A PRECIOUS GIFT

> Oh, the places you'll go! You'll be on your way up! You'll be seeing great sights! You'll join the high-fliers who soar to high heights.

Dr. Seuss, Oh, the Places You'll Go

CHAPTER 5

Mirrors of the Soul

In the same way every book is different, what a book means to each and every person can be different.

Where were you when you read the book? Who were you with? Were you happy or sad? Energetic or tired? Are there any evocative smells or sounds that rush back when you think of that book?

THE LITTLE BOOK OF BOOKS

> **Books are the mirrors of the soul.**
>
> Virginia Woolf

MIRRORS OF THE SOUL

> "
>
> One glance at a book and you hear the voice of another person, perhaps someone dead for 1,000 years. To read is to voyage through time.
>
> "
>
> *Carl Sagan*

THE LITTLE BOOK OF BOOKS

> You can never get a cup of tea large enough or a book long enough to suit me.

C.S. Lewis

MIRRORS OF THE SOUL

> If one cannot enjoy reading a book over and over again, there is no use in reading it at all.

Oscar Wilde

THE LITTLE BOOK OF BOOKS

>> There is more treasure in books than in all the pirate's loot on Treasure Island. <<

Walt Disney

> And read…
> read all the time…
> read as a matter of
> principle, as a matter
> of self-respect.
> Read as a nourishing
> staple of life.

David McCullough Jr.

THE LITTLE BOOK OF BOOKS

> **Books were my pass to personal freedom.**

Oprah Winfrey

MIRRORS OF THE SOUL

> More than at any other time, when I hold a beloved book in my hand my limitations fall from me, my spirit is free.

Helen Keller

> Reading is escape, and the opposite of escape; it's a way to make contact with reality after a day of making things up, and it's a way of making contact with someone else's imagination after a day that's all too real.

Nora Ephron

MIRRORS OF THE SOUL

> For some of us, books are as important as almost anything else on earth. What a miracle it is that out of these small, flat, rigid squares of paper unfolds world after world after world, worlds that sing to you, comfort and quiet or excite you. Books help us understand who we are and how we are to behave. They show us what community and friendship mean; they show us how to live and die.

Anne Lamott

THE LITTLE BOOK OF BOOKS

> What a blessing it is to love books as I love them; to be able to converse with the dead, and to live amidst the unreal!

Thomas Babington Macaulay

MIRRORS OF THE SOUL

> "Reading is an exercise in empathy; an exercise in walking in someone else's shoes for a while."

Malorie Blackman

> Maybe this is why we read, and why in moments of darkness we return to books: to find words for what we already know.

Alberto Manguel

> The unread story is not a story; it is little black marks on wood pulp. The reader, reading it, makes it live: a live thing, a story.

Ursula K. LeGuin

> Reading is an act of civilization; it's one of the greatest acts of civilization because it takes the free raw material of the mind and builds castles of possibilities.

Ben Okri

MIRRORS OF THE SOUL

> Books are mirrors: you only see in them what you already have inside you.

Carlos Ruiz Zafón,
The Shadow of the Wind

> Reading makes immigrants of us all. It takes us away from home, but more important, it finds homes for us everywhere.

Jean Rhys

> The best moments in reading are when you come across something – a thought, a feeling, a way of looking at things – which you had thought special and particular to you. Now here it is, set down by someone else, a person you have never met, someone even who is long dead. And it is as if a hand has come out and taken yours.

Alan Bennett, The History Boys

> If you cannot read all your books... fondle them, peer into them, let them fall open where they will, read from the first sentence that arrests the eye, set them back on the shelves with your own hands, arrange them on your own plan so that you at least know where they are. Let them be your friends; let them, at any rate, be your acquaintances.

Winston Churchill

MIRRORS OF THE SOUL

> To acquire the habit of reading is to construct for yourself a refuge from almost all the miseries of life.

W. Somerset Maugham

> Read, read, read. Read everything — trash, classics, good and bad, and see how they do it. Just like a carpenter who works as an apprentice and studies the master. Read! You'll absorb it. Then write. If it's good, you'll find out. If it's not, throw it out of the window.

William Faulkner

> Books give a soul to the universe, wings to the mind, flight to the imagination, and life to everything.

Plato

> When I think about how I understand my role as citizen, setting aside being president... the most important stuff I've learned I think I've learned from novels.

Barack Obama

MIRRORS OF THE SOUL

> 66
>
> We are such stuff as dreams are made on, and our little life is rounded with a sleep.
>
> 99
>
> *William Shakespeare*, **The Tempest**

CHAPTER
6

Famous Lines from Famous Books

What follows are some of my favourite lines from well-known books I have read.

Hopefully you'll find some pixie dust, and, if you do, don't procrastinate – make a list of your own from the books you love.

> I declare after all there is no enjoyment like reading! How much sooner one tires of anything than of a book! When I have a house of my own, I shall be miserable if I have not an excellent library.

Jane Austen, Pride and Prejudice

FAMOUS LINES FROM FAMOUS BOOKS

> If you only read the books that everyone else is reading, you can only think what everyone else is thinking.

Haruki Murakami, Norwegian Wood

> # Who controls the past controls the future. Who controls the present controls the past.

George Orwell, Nineteen Eighty-Four

FAMOUS LINES FROM FAMOUS BOOKS

> It is better to know one book intimately than a hundred superficially.

Donna Tartt, The Secret History

> What really knocks me out is a book that, when you're all done reading it, you wish the author that wrote it was a terrific friend of yours and you could call him up on the phone whenever you felt like it. That doesn't happen much, though.

J.D. Salinger, The Catcher In The Rye

FAMOUS LINES FROM FAMOUS BOOKS

> Some of these things are true and some of them lies. But they are all good stories.

Hilary Mantel, Wolf Hall

THE LITTLE BOOK OF BOOKS

> Until I feared I would lose it, I never loved to read. One does not love breathing.

Harper Lee, To Kill A Mockingbird

FAMOUS LINES FROM FAMOUS BOOKS

> "The magic is only in what books say, how they stitched the patches of the universe together into one garment for us."

Ray Bradbury, Fahrenheit 451

> A classic is a successful book that has survived the reaction of the next period or generation. Then it's safe, like a style in architecture or furniture. It's acquired a picturesque dignity to take the place of its fashion.

F. Scott Fitzgerald, The Beautiful and Damned

FAMOUS LINES FROM FAMOUS BOOKS

> All the world is made of faith, and trust, and pixie dust.

J.M Barrie, Peter Pan

> A man, after he has brushed off the dust and chips of his life, will have left only the hard, clean questions: Was it good or was it evil? Have I done well – or ill?

John Steinbeck, East of Eden

FAMOUS LINES FROM FAMOUS BOOKS

> I am no bird; and no net ensnares me: I am a free human being with an independent will, which I now exert to leave you.

Charlotte Brontë, Jane Eyre

THE LITTLE BOOK OF BOOKS

> Some books are so familiar that reading them is like being home again.

Louisa May Alcott, Little Women

FAMOUS LINES FROM FAMOUS BOOKS

> As I left China farther and farther behind, I looked out of the window and saw a great universe beyond the plane's silver wing. I took one more glance over my past life, then turned to the future. I was eager to embrace the world.

Jung Chang, Wild Swans

> 'Why did you do all this for me?' he asked. 'I don't deserve it. I've never done anything for you.'
> 'You have been my friend,' replied Charlotte. 'That in itself is a tremendous thing.'

E.B. White, Charlotte's Web

FAMOUS LINES FROM FAMOUS BOOKS

> It is nothing to die; it is dreadful not to live.

Victor Hugo, Les Miserables

THE LITTLE BOOK OF BOOKS

> All happy families are alike; each unhappy family is unhappy in its own way.

Leo Tolstoy, Anna Karenina

FAMOUS LINES FROM FAMOUS BOOKS

> "Memories warm you up from the inside. But they also tear you apart."

Haruki Murakami, Kafka on the Shore

> It was the best of times, it was the worst of times, it was the age of wisdom, it was the age of foolishness, it was the epoch of belief, it was the epoch of incredulity, it was the season of Light, it was the season of Darkness, it was the spring of hope, it was the winter of despair…

Charles Dickens, A Tale of Two Cities

FAMOUS LINES FROM FAMOUS BOOKS

> **Why, sometimes, I've believed as many as six impossible things before breakfast.**

Lewis Carroll, Through the Looking Glass

> If you have the guts to be yourself, other people'll pay your price.

John Updike, Rabbit, Run

FAMOUS LINES FROM FAMOUS BOOKS

> Generally, by the time you are Real, most of your hair has been loved off, and your eyes drop out and you get loose in the joints and very shabby. But these things don't matter at all, because once you are Real you can't be ugly, except to people who don't understand.

Margery Williams, The Velveteen Rabbit

THE LITTLE BOOK OF BOOKS

> # Love is the longing for the half of ourselves we have lost.

Milan Kundera,
The Unbearable Lightness of Being

FAMOUS LINES FROM FAMOUS BOOKS

> My advice is, never do tomorrow what you can do today. Procrastination is the thief of time.

Charles Dickens, David Copperfield

> It is only with the heart that one can see rightly; what is essential is invisible to the eye.

Antoine de Saint-Exupéry,
The Little Prince

FAMOUS LINES FROM FAMOUS BOOKS

'And now,' cried Max, 'let the wild rumpus start!'

Maurice Sendak,
Where the Wild Things Are

THE LITTLE BOOK OF BOOKS

> Memories, even your most precious ones, fade surprisingly quickly. But I don't go along with that. The memories I value most, I don't ever see them fading.

Kazuo Ishiguro, Never Let Me Go

FAMOUS LINES FROM FAMOUS BOOKS

> But wherever they go, and whatever happens to them on the way, in that enchanted place on the top of the Forest a little boy and his Bear will always be playing.

A.A. Milne,
The House At Pooh Corner

> The old man was dreaming about the lions.

Ernest Hemingway,
The Old Man and the Sea